FIVE TERRACES

Five Terraces

Ann Fisher-Wirth

WIND PUBLICATIONS

First edition

International Standard Book Number 1893239446
Library of Congress Control Number 2005927989

Front cover photograph © Yann Arthus-Bertrand / Altitude

Acknowledgments

The author thanks the editors of the following journals in which these poems appeared or will appear, sometimes in different forms:

Center, "Aporia"
The Connecticut Review, "Sphinx, Star-Gazer. Mountain" (Part II of "Yoga in the Mornings, Poetry in the Afternoons," in collaboration with Beth Ann Fennelly), "Rain," "In That Kitchen"
Flyway, "After Many Years She Returns to the Stage in a Play by Tennessee Williams," "After Twenty Years," "Blesser (Fr.): To Wound, to Hurt; to Offend, to Injure; to Wring, to Shock, to Gall," "Kisses," "Trinket's Brag"
Iris: A Journal About Women, "In Crescent"
The Merton Seasonal, "But the Bodhisattva Comes"
NILAS (Nature in Legend and Story), "Five Terraces" (as "In Berkeley")
Poetry International, "At McClure's Beach, Point Reyes National Seashore, California"
Runes, "Snabbt Jagar Stormen Våra År"
Wind, "Devotions," "Sideways"
The Yalobusha Review, "A Fable"

"Rain" won the 2004 Rita Dove Poetry Award at the Salem College Center for Women Writers; "October" was a finalist in the contest. "But the Bodhisattva Comes" received Honorable Mention in the 2004 Thomas Merton Poetry of the Sacred Contest. "Walking Wu Wei's Scroll *'Le Grand Fleuve à perte de vue'*" received Honorable Mention in the 2005 Center for Book Arts Chapbook Contest.

"The Trinket Poems" appeared in chapbook form as runner-up in the 2003 Quentin R. Howard Poetry Chapbook Competiton and is published as *Wind 90: The Chapbook. Edition: Dana Sonnenschein and Ann Fisher-Wirth.*

"Walking Wu Wei's Scroll *'Le Grande Fleuve à perte de vue,'*" "Mississippi," "Marriage," and "Having No Choice, I Welcome You" appear as a chapbook online on *The Drunken Boat.*

Many have helped to make this book. I am especially grateful to Beth Ann Fennelly and Peter Wirth, who read and critiqued many of these poems at various stages, and to Jessica Fisher and Gabriel Scala, who worked their magic shaping the manuscript. It is a great honor to have four such brilliant and generous readers. My warm thanks also to Diane Lockward, who sent me to Wind, and to my editor Charlie Hughes.

A residency at the Mesa Refuge in Point Reyes Station, California, and grants from the Mississippi Arts Commission and the University of Mississippi gave me time to write the poems in this book. I am thankful for their generous support.

For those I love

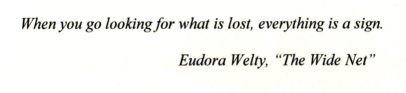

When you go looking for what is lost, everything is a sign.

Eudora Welty, "The Wide Net"

Contents

III

IV

V

VI

VII

I

Walking Wu Wei's Scroll
"Le Grand Fleuve à perte de vue"

You could be the man in the small house making tea,
or one of the friends fishing off the footbridge over the river.

* * *

You could be that aspen, that cedar—
or the woman we do not see, who spins thread or boils silkworms
in the house below the boulder, the house
of which we see
an upper roof corner, and another, then the rocks surround it.

Out of silence, the brimming lake, spills the waterfall.
Behind mountains, other mountains fade
until we cannot tell
what's stone, what's cloud,
and what the mark of time upon the silk.

      And look, here someone rides home—
or is it a squiggle—
up the path to a terraced house.
Then a village fading in fog,
on the watery side of the mountain.

                *   *   *

Somewhere in those houses, a lover turns to his beloved.
Somewhere else, a child cries.

                    But the cries
of their pain or pleasure are lost in the fog . . .
though not how a man's hands caress
and caress a blue bowl, turning and warming it
between his fingers—
a bowl in which a fish, now dizzy with circling, swims.

Now they go down to boats we do not see.
The merest wisps of pine trees dot the waters.

* * *

And what do *you* want? Where is your house?
Or do you walk among the rocks, beneath the trees?

Oh, me, if I can't be the fish,
swimming giddily round and round as my orange fins
flashed and his hands warmed my waters,
then I'd like to be the fog,
and lay my touch down
on every crack and crevice, every pine,
every boulder—and give the villagers sleep.

Time mars the silk:
a few spots and stains, as if smoke or tears.
Then rushes, fishing junks, elegant curved sails,
facing into the open waters.

        *   *   *

Now we have come to the place,
my love,
where I must lay you down.
Only a few hair-thin scribbles of boats endure,
and the mountains
whose edges cannot be distinguished from shadow.

Ah, the courage to leave something empty.
To wait, and wait,
                        and wait,
as the hair-thin fishing boats float and wait

                till at last, the world (as we call it)
reconstitutes itself in the solemnity of boulders.
As on both sides of the scroll—
to east, to west; to right, to left—
solidity cups fog, or as two hands cup the silence where a face was.

            *   *   *

And here again, a village, two men on a bridge,
the torque and slow fluidity of trees.

Brushstrokes black on gray
define the ridges of the mountains.

7

Where would I be in this? I would be anywhere.

Each thing singular, each thing perfect,
fog and water
and tree and rocks, the fish that swims in its bowl,
the blood that swims in the bowl of the body.
Entrails, cilia—and here, toward the left side of the scroll,
the faintest touches of pink:

Why? As if dawn is coming?

*   *   *

No climax, no conclusion.

We begin with such solidity: large trees, boulders,
thickest and densest at the beginning.
Midway through the scroll, the emptiness is greatest,
the *brume* thickest. Then, moving left, the solidity returns.

But no: moving left, the emptiness returns.
The village fades away once more, at the left side of the scroll,

and we're in fog, in swirl and fade,
with only the faintest shadows to say "mountain"
and slashes to say "foreground: trees,"
or maybe "boats," or maybe just "slashes."

8

Here and there, all facing the same direction,
fishing boats near and far: alone, together.

And half the people walking this scroll
here at the Grand Palais on the 21st of June
move left to right, and half move right to left.
It doesn't matter.

* * *

But the faintest pink in the houses to the left—
                                   is that dawn,
or has someone lit some tiny lanterns?

The Trinket Poems

It's all of the gods, there's nothing else worth writing of.
They are the same men [and women] they always were—
but fallen.

William Carlos Williams, Kora in Hell

Blesser: (Fr.) To Wound, to Hurt; to Offend, to Injure; to Wring, to Shock, to Gall

If *to wound* is *to bless* they are blessed,
Trinket and Celeste, these two drunk, aging floozies—
one needs makeup to look aging and the other,
the desperate courage of aging to play a floozy—
they are blessed as they kneel there with the gallon
jug of Tokay, the crystal wine decanter, and their
loss-induced vision of the Virgin Mary. Oh I know
it's false etymology but think about it: doesn't what
brings you to your knees gut-punched, or makes you
sit on the toilet as your lover lies sleeping
and scratch bright welts along your thighs ·
with the paring knife, the fingernail scissors,
or drops you fetal to the forest floor because you've
run so far away from home, sobbing *mother, father,*
help me—doesn't the day you stand in the empty house
of the family you destroyed, sent your children
like dandelion seedpods spinning off into the golden
canyons of grief far beyond their small as yet imaginings—
doesn't even this somehow bless them, bless you?
Hard to speak of, even now. You will pray the kind
earth to swallow you.
         Ah, but the god doesn't care.
Trinket turns to the Virgin when the bright one
spurns her. As for you—
that long-ago April you kindled like leaf fire.

After Many Years She Returns to the Stage in "The Mutilated," by Tennessee Williams

She runs her fingers over the cheek and down the throat
and slender chest of this boy
fuck age-appropriate
fuck that she's a professor it's not specific to him anyway
she arches her body against him and moans
when he orders her be my slave and God she has
climbed inside delirium
                            between scenes she
sits by herself in the theatre envying the students
like a pack of puppies with each other's bodies
last time they made love her husband
whispered to her holding her close
her face in his hands   *throat   wrist   breast*
reminded her of her magic words as a child
for the white meat where the blood beat close to the surface
to shame her

                Why did she give it up

Why did she let it stop

It's 1964 she's
passing the white-flowered bushes in front of Little Bridges
that accost her with their wild sweet rotting meat smell
night and joy she is big strides
coming in tights from the improv group
where everyone sleeps with everyone sooner or later
and so why not touch   caress
let the audience watch

16

them burn   lithe arcs and turns   oh foolish
bound by the body and wanting to be fire
in the dance she
throws herself down on the stage
so hard she leaves bruises all over
her back in ecstasy and thrashes
for the boy who burns the paint off his dorm room walls

She walks fully clothed on April into the midnight cold Pacific
licks salt and honey off the bright god's clavicle
there's a boy who calls her a holy whore
no she never takes money but sometimes thinks why not
it's what I want to do anyway

                    It's what I want to do anyway

In a week it will be over
she has stirred her life to the bottom of the pot
tasted those years again when her hair flowed to her shoulders
when any road to any end might run and sometimes did
when her hands shook with the constant cigarettes
there is no happy ending to this drama
but on stage tonight a moment touching his face his hair
gold   red gold   and skin like snow
like sunlight on snow   she steps into the fire

Facing the Audience

Tonight the sea of faces an arm's-length
away as Trinket goes into her tremor
in front of the park bench, and she wants
to be a seagull, raucous, screaming,
she'll eat any trash, Trinket doesn't give a shit
if you see her come. How these kids
parade their bodies. My Celeste lies right down
in the green room, skirt to her hips, thighs spread,
guys watching or playing cards or eating
their Taco Bell, and goes into her
aah-aah-aah-aaah relaxation quiver,
body trembling, pelvis pounding. Oh how
we want to be loved, my mother would drive
eight hours to Claremont to see me act
for an audience of thirteen in some
pretentious play, and tell me then, *you were perfect.*

Aporia

Her thighs through the slit of red kimono
glimmer and shift on the ghostly iron
bedstead. Outside the tattered lace curtain
rain falls, still, rain, as she arches a foot
back and forth, idly, flexing, extending
her toes with their pearly pink nails in time
with Bing Crosby on the radio, "White
Christmas," though here on the streets the sailors
stagger and weave toward the Café Bohème
as she lounges, smoke rising, a single
cigarette. The god has taken her breast.
Carve her shame on the walls, still the question
remains, what space for the sacred
in this century? …The actress playing
Trinket, the aging woman whose fingers
never stop moving over the bedposts,
the chenille, who cannot draw hard enough
on the stage non-nicotine cigarette,
her warm breast fills her hand every time her
hand flies to her chest to mark its absence.
So what is missing, after all? Well, what
if the shut door opened in this seedy
New Orleans hotel room, what if the womb
of the actress playing Trinket blossomed
again because the bright god entered,
Mardi Gras beads dropping from her stunned hands?

Gel Room

Above the main stage, on the way to Trinket's
bedroom, the gel room contains colored plastic sheets
to put over lights. It's a place of transformations.

Better check my ass in the mirror
to know what they'd see if they were looking—
the guys in the gel room where I change
from patio pants to silk kimono—
the dresser Eric, the Pious Queen, Death
as Jack in Black, and two drunk Sailors.
Never worn a thong in my life.
So I'm stripping down for the undergrads
who turn to watch the walls as I fumble
with pink silk tap pants, camisole, my ankle
slave chain breaks again, and here I am, white
cheeks I hope to God are firm enough
if they see them, rushing to
Trinket's room to be abused again.
I'm old enough to be my Sailor's grandma.
But when this boy who will never be my lover—
when he slumps against me drunk just before we
stagger into the bedroom for the sex scene—
well I lean into him then, when we're our
daily selves we barely speak in the green room,
but once he's Slim who will hurt me, and I'm
Trinket who will flaunt for him, press her
whole body against him—I take comfort
from him then, this 21-year-old
Texan with a brother named Millennius
and another brother named Felix,
I lean into his warm armpit and ribcage
with the trust of the long married.

Trinket's Brag

Bruno: "Ever done it in an alley?"

No but Trinket's done it
                    In her mother Mary's bed
                              On her mother Julie's floor
          In front of her mother Francesca's full-length mirror

              At the Rodeo Drive-in in Albuquerque
                      In Marilee's bunk in Savannah
With Natalie's brother and sister in Santa Fe

On the sand at Coral Gables
                              On the stones by Dana Point

Trinket's done it screaming   Laughing   She's done it
       So tenderly   You could set the rain
         And a baby's heartbeat by it

               Trinket's done it
With the Mayor and the President of the International Trade Mart

With a collie   A candle   A pinecone
         Done it burning   Bored   Bleeding

Done it when she knew it was right and done it
           When she knew it was wrong

Done it with her five strong fingers

With her Father in a dream once
Lucent he came to her
Through the valley of ash

With her one and one and one and one and yet again one true love and more

And sometimes Trinket's gone down
To the river of men
And lain on her pallet in rags or naked
Then the bright
Gods and
Cockroaches
Flowed through her door

Speak These Lines

*Trinket: "He will be beautiful! Perfect! —Perhaps he'll be
kind, even, so kind I can tell him about my—mutilation."*

Speak these lines. Don't look toward the audience.
Say them on your knees, face the wall above the bar
where stagehands have painted a field of stars,
a galaxy; say them into the whirling field of fire
where stagehands have laid their handprints also,
blue, white, golden, double handprints like birds; say them
into this black, stained and scarred field of paint where human labor
hammers and planes and nails its sets together, look closely.
The coffee is not coffee, wine is not wine—but the wafers
are wafers, and smoke really does rise from the avid ritual,
the mouth and fingers dance that is your Scene One cigarette.
Say these lines which are foolish, which are the heart's
nakedness, proudly, as if the galaxy whirled and
kindled through your scarred, stained darkness also.

Who Will Be the Richest? Who Will Love Me Most? Who Will Make Me Speak His Name in Tongues?

I ache for you when you're not near but do not tell
                                    anyone about you
                    La vida es sueño
        My death prepares in me
                                            like the bloodspot of an egg
                    and the heart begs for anything but mercy
        Piques   Carreaux   Trèfles   Coeurs
                                    my Sailor laid the cards out
                    laid the cards out
                            each suit an old lover…

Tell the truth   Once
                                    I sat all night in the California June
                    with just the screen door shut, listening
        to the crickets in the lemon
                                            tree outside
                    the bamboo creaking with growing
        I read my book in the shadows
                            cast by the single lamp
                    nested in a swarm
                    of shadows—

Till you came
                            arching my spine, making
                    my elbows, collarbone, hipbones, taut with warning
        You came to where
                            the screen door was shut, locked

24

and then you were inside
like turning a glove
                    inside out the moment
        you finally make inside outside
                cleanly.

Small Interlude Where She Argues

So easily shamed, aren't we, Trinket?
Women our age, how happy they sometimes
say they are to pass beyond desire, wombs
and breasts like docile children, they learn Greek,
climb mountains. And I think ho ho I'm lost,
the jutting cheekbones, warm flat muscular
body of this boy, beauty like my sons' friends'
when they're here on vacation and sleeping, all
ribs and hairy knees and sloping shoulderblades...

Hang on to the real, I tell myself,
meaning, I know who I am—

                                But Trinket,
when you're kneeling, his hand knotting your hair
as you gaze up at him pretending
he didn't really mean to spill the coffee—
when you're wiping it up then caressing
his ankle, his calf, as he tightens his grip
to force your head back—you know if you could
see yourself you'd cringe, you'd sicken, hunger
so raw in that visibly sagging jawline,
gaunt throat, those veined, trembling fingers.

You want the god to lift you up.
—to forgive you the raddled flesh you can't help
wrapping like mangy furs around the queen.

Small Interlude, Still, Where She Argues

Hang on to the real, she said to herself,
this is getting full of gods and Sailors.
You can't just admit they're college kids,
you're an English professor and mother of five
slumming in satin, fake fur, and grease paint?

                    But gods and Sailors have ribs
and sloping shoulderblades. You cannot know
the blessed ones except in mortal flesh
with mortal longing. Say Christ like any
long-haired friend of your sons walked into the room,
would you fall to your knees or ask Him
to help you change the unreachable light bulb?
Say Beth Ann, commenting on the play,
refers to "the pointy-headed boy who was so mean
to Trinket," and suddenly you see yourselves
with these undazzled eyes, does that make you
any the less Trinket,
or him any the less Trinket's Sailor?

Of Trinket, of Mary

When you stand by the radio after
the Sailor spurns you, and because it is
silent, the cathedral empty, you know
the Christ child has been born, your hand wanders
to that absence as if He seeks the thin blue
milk, the veined orb beneath the cloth of stars—
As your Sailor sleeps his brutal sleep you speak
of the Christ child, his blind sweet hands
fumbling beneath the robes of his mother,
and Trinket, I had that. Rocking or
in bed, or carrying my babies beneath
my pink *ruana* as I walked hours
and hours through the summer woods, their lips
pulling down the starry river, I had that.

Shore Leave

In her dream he flings the cards into a furl,
a flash of light on plum-purple wings
across the high white room where she has just
finished sleeping, finished dreaming of the ocean's
doom and dazzle. He flings the cards out,
swooping, rising, then catches them
into a waterfall. Oh she is young again.
Years spray like mist from his spinning fingers.

But the sea road is his, hers the red gold memory
of his cheek beneath her ring-decked fingers.
In this room at the top of the stairs
where the sad mattress blanches and wakes
beneath the one-breasted moon,
she has only the boys' choir on the radio,
only the candles, the contingencies of roses,
and Mardi Gras beads looped over the mirror.

There Is a Diary Open to the Words

Forgive me.

       I gather a solitary terror around me
the way you draw together the scarlet
kimono, wrapping the smooth embroidered
panels tight across your breast, and then stoop
to the mirror, unwrapping one side,
the heart side, just enough to see the pink
silk camisole. Is there damage there?
Dear diary, dear diary...

                Trinket,
you've become my dance, today I cannot
go forward, last night when Arlene wanted
to do my makeup I just stood there weeping,
tears making me rivers of soot and leaves.

"These Our Actors, As I Foretold You . . ."

So Kat fell in love at First Dress with a guy
in the tech room. Now she's radiant but
she can't pee, we used to call it Honeymoon
Fever. Wistaria thickens today
above the porch swing, and dust trails its furry
feet along my unswept floorboards.
The play is over, the scene struck. The Pious
Queen has lost his tiara. My Sailor's
gone off to his girlfriend in Texas.
Priscilla who traced her nipples and howled
like a banshee whore in Scene Four is back
at Blue Marlin waiting tables. Actors
break our hearts, they rejoice in the bright
world in their hands then watch it vanish.
I want life to be kind to them, my *compadres*
and *comadres* at Tennessee Williams's
Silver Dollar Hotel, these kids who flaunt
and flame, who do not sleep, these angels
and divas who belt it out in the green room,
mocking the words to every love song.
While I've been dazzled my yard's sprung up
with colt's-foot, clover. And Trinket's alone
in her room once more, fiddling with the dials,
trying to raise a station on the radio . . .

It Was Like Being Alive Twice

Now, heart, it is time to be quiet.
The voices have other work to do, someone needs them—

A woman in Great Falls, perhaps,
a blue-haired woman turning round and round
in the calm of her life
while blackbirds rise from shorn wheat fields,
touching her throat with shaking fingers—

All girls who rock themselves on dorm room beds—

A young mother in Metairie. She stirs spaghetti sauce,
diapers her babies, still and always grieving
her Sailor lover's death—
                    Suddenly he comes one final time.
The air
grows tight and hot above her shoulders.

Hardest of all to say
                    Yes

Hardest of all not to fall on her knees—
To say *Go since you must go, I carry you always.*
I know
that you have been here . . .

My Darling Heart —
This comes with all
my love. Another box will
arrive soon — nothing much
except I love mine & I want
you to have one —
Happy Birthday — Love
Mom &
Dad

"Sonoma Valley" by Crabtree & Evelyn

We've taken the furniture, porcelain,
jewelry, everything but your photographs
and little crystal Buddha. Still you lie there,
lie there… And I pray for your release
from the tyranny of seasons. You open your eyes,
the nurse spoons liquids, but you don't move,
no blink or whisper, like some bivalve
you just shut down more tightly.
                 Mother, love, by now your dying
bores me. And for this I think you'd hate me.
Off I've gone to play dress-up with the kids,
to dream about sex and the raunchier angels—
I want sweetness. Didn't you? I want lyrical notes
of "Sonoma Valley," hours and hours
in a honeyed torpor when every petal opens
and opens—or as, on Friday night,
just before the Sailor turned on her forever,
Trinket raked his cheek with peony-lacquered
fingers, wishing she dared rip sweet scarlet berries
from the bone branch, pack her nails with bright
flesh dirt… So I sprayed the cologne I took from you
on the female roués and denizens of the Café
Bohème, the Silver Dollar—on Tiger, Celeste,
The Woman at the Bar—copiously every night
I sprayed your cologne all over my own wrists,
throat, hair, my Trinket breasts, in our good-show-
feel-hot-girls ritual, because we may come
to where you are but for now the shapes
still shift for us, blood still rises in our gorges,
and Tiger who seems shy, a little lonely,

would glance every night at the empty makeup shelf
in the green room and pantomime joy, spreading
her arms out wide like a beauty queen, punching up
the Southern accent, *Why thank you so much.*
You brought me the most beautiful delicious flowahs.

Answers to April

Every year since childhood your piercing greens
stir my heart, constrict the bone
cage of my throat, you flaunt the tenderness
that troubles me in his touch   her touch   his touch
redbuds sprung to their branches
like blossoms of fever.

*

Grackles lift and sink
above the broken-shingled roof of my drunk neighbour
where all rots and teems and swells, derelict, dies
and blossoms and I want to too
just cast off this skin, molt, all raw and moist
oh look at the aging woman
dreaming about the cheekbones of boys
April you are shaming me.

*

You do not grow old in me
your cruelty does not abate
they tell me past the change we grow serene
but the moon still pulls the milky tilth of me
I blush   flush
like the petals of dogwoods
opening out today all over town
from wooden to sexual, each with its bite or burn
blessing it
with the mark of its corruption   yes   yes
I would not be carried
unmarred   untorn   to the river.

Butoh: "Bird"

How silly you are, Trinket. The world
is infinite. Leave your room by the spiral
staircase, leave the ghostly bedstead and
the half-smoked cigarette, Mardi Gras beads
iridescent, gold, blue as the veins of
your hands, on the mirror. Take your scar—
what poets call the proud flesh. Wear it.
Pain is infinite.
                              In the Grove
during yoga today, Michele taught us "The Bird,"
a butoh dance move. Mouth opened, eyes closed,
spring's first grass and dogwoods all around her,
her body twisted, spine extended, arm-
wings stiffened, rose slowly, slowly, till she
clawed frozen at heaven—then sank down
into the egg again, rested there, grass-washed,
sun-licked. Watching, I thought, that's *your* dance,
Trinket, when you spasm by the park bench,
when your mouth opens but no sound comes out,
that rictus and writhe, wild with the bitter-old
winter-cold hunger for love—that "Bird,"
dance form born of the dying—

In Crescent

The bloodwall thickens
and everyone I have loved
begins to ripen within my body.
A quiet time: the house
curls in upon itself, enfolds
the sleeping children; the daisy
shuts its petals, and their lashes are wet
with the mercy of sleep.

Summer's grasses
are long, so long
that we seem to move through water.
Children again, we clamor, Mother
may I, mother may I? And she
by the elm in shadow, whose belly
catches moonlight: Come
as you will, I will hold you,
I am warm, all steps
lead where I am hidden.

And so inch forward toward that
teeming bed
where we all lie down together.

Reading Dinner

we called it, when we'd each bring a book, prop it open under the edge of a plate or balance a salt shaker on the pages, and read while we cut our meat, passed the sugar, scooped out peas or mashed potatoes. We sat at the cherrywood dropleaf table, in the alcove with yellow organza curtains, turning the pages of a mystery, or history homework, or *Glamor* magazine, and ate in silence. Oh, sometimes the phone rang, that ugly brown wall phone with its long snaky cord that got dirty and tangled, that you could pull to its full length to go whisper in the hall, but then our mother would say, "Dear, call back when you've finished your dinner."

Sometimes the cups and the sorrow would be very small, and our mother would just sit, silent. We were near her. Near her. Mid-American cooking, nothing special, but every night we ate together, even when there was nothing to say, when to begin to talk would have meant starting down a black staircase, backward, still gesturing with the hands.

So those winters after my father's death, my sister and I helped our mother through those long Berkeley dinner hours, reading, passing the salt, our hands warm if they brushed each other. And outside, dark coming on early in the roses he had planted, in the wormy apple trees, the azaleas and fijoas. Dark coming on early across the Bay, fog spilt through the Golden Gate, little drops of rain beading the window glass, licking the spiky leaves of the olive tree.

Moth

The girl I once was
stared through grief and fever
at a devil clad in orange, some earth-arranger.
He waited beneath the pines
as they tucked my newborn's ashes
beside my father's grave, grim joke
or grace: *Watch over her, Papa.*
Papa you died in time to spare you shame.

Three weeks later milk came in,
all down the front of my new white dress.
I gave myself to scalding waters,
pounded my head on the walls of showers.
Oh I was death's girl,
sure to poison anything I loved,
any sweet cock or baby that came near me.

*

When my other children came,
a half-light dogged them. They learned to want her too,
the dead sister who made me a mother,
who made me stop, sometimes,
and go quiet in hallways, as if my arms
were full of blankets for someone who was not them,
who slept down a long corridor
in a room where curtains billowed
in watery sunlight.
                              Or when I
read to them at night and their sweet

bodies and hair grew sticky with summer as they
sprawled all over me, there was a moth
at the window, a soft moon-splotched moth battering at the window,
and that moth could never get in
no matter how they opened
and opened—

Bacalao

How the flamenco singer's voice cracked
that long-ago night, when I was first a wife,
in the limestone caverns of Granada—
cracked, and broke into the no-man's-land,
the screech and quaver of the duende,
the music that happens *after* the voice is shattered—
He, the ancient widower of the Gypsy Queen,
held his bacalao to my lips
and insisted "taste, taste," the fish
already spit-moistened, hard as a board,
rank with salt: what was he to me—
the evening's entertainment   drunkard   consort
to a royalty I'll never see or be?
In those white caverns my husband
lifted a beer to the tour guide
as the dancers stamped their feet and twirled,
spines like flames, scarlet ruffles
flared around them, and till long past midnight,
the widower of the Gypsy Queen
smacked his guitar and yowled.
The tour guide, the waiters,
kept muttering to us, *El es muy especial,*
el es un maestro del flamenco—
and he was, this man with the wail
and cracked black shoes
who, summoned, lashed, tried to outrace dawn.
My whole being seeks that magic.

43

Devotions

Every night, every morning, she holds
her finger beneath the baby's nostril
and waits for the warm slide of breath
across her finger, the moist, infinitesimal
fluttering. She hangs prostrate on a sign:
a grunt, a fart, that sweet involuntary sucking
where the lower lip vanishes. *If it rises
and falls, if it rises and falls...* She cannot
believe the child will live. She watches
her daughter's chest, the small waves
of her breathing—
                It's 1973. They're so poor
it's a crisis when she breaks a jar of honey.
A lemon tree spreads at their bedroom window,
and at night, around the patio the young
husband made, driving to the chaparral
for stones then lugging them back
in the old VW van, bamboo groans with growing.
Let's not speak of what's wrong between them,
this husband who's so anxious and thin
he can suck his belly like a cavern
to his backbone, this wife who stayed in bed
all spring, scarcely daring to lift her head
every time the spotting started, since that day
in the mountains at four months when she bled
and the nurse at the emergency clinic
told her, Yup, I heard of a woman who woke
after a week of safety and the whole
bed was a puddle of blood.

             Let's just say
poverty and terror can break a marriage.
Let's not speak of the sorrow
this child and her sister and brother
will inherit; instead, listen to the story
their mother tells them, how all the babies
line up in the sky by the baby ladder,
and slide down when they hear their future
parents say, This one… This one… This one…
How they are the chosen babies of all the world.

Here

What is this rain that greets us
                    as I step off the airplane, as we drive,
                                    what is this gift of cold, here
                where blackberries ripen, how
                                can flesh consent this way and who am I
        in this thunderstorm here
                            where the potters' field is,
                    where my bones become unfleshed, his wet
                                wet hair and beard upon me, am I
                    on rocks? am I up against a tree?

He will be my husband
            we lie

                                            drenched
                        and muddy
                    avoiding his parents' house
        with its velvet couch
                                    fine wine and candlesticks
                where they worry about the storm: are they okay?
                        is he driving safely?
                                    but here beneath the trees
        slick like toads we lie rejoicing

                                            Here
We don't need, yet, to step
                                    back inside houses, here grief is
            not, yet, the rain sluices
                down on me, on his chill flesh,
                            his drenched flannel shirt, his collarbone
                    still with its warm pulse, what's dry?
Nothing, nothing, laughing, so
                        in the woods where people won't come
                where people won't come except us in the thunder.

46

A Fable

Why try to explain?
She walked outside
into a field of stars
where he stood waiting.
At the black edge of the pine trees,
she married the bear.

Tonight smoke rises
from the village fires.
They beat pots to ward off evil.

After Twenty Years

He doesn't quite know what to do with me.
I lie beside him twitching in the bed
and he says, "Is it your leg again?"
Oh no my love, it's another cramping.
Year after year I've eaten him away
with the tyranny of niceness, *Now now*
calm down, no rage, no negativity...
that American wife thing I've done
to him, whom I could barely look at once
without fainting, throat tight with all
the crazy words that flung themselves like silken
spinnerets against him, who caught hold
and saved me—

And now we have spun this shimmering
wide net which is dawn with cardinals singing
in the privet, which is our white bed
beneath the window, pillows rumpled, quilt
heavy and warm with the valleys of cats,
which is his leg with its bony knee pressed
into me, my leg thrown over his, soft
cock fluttering sleepily in my hand, now
his furred belly warms my back, he's my bear—

But I miss the teeth that would grip my throat
once, the blood on the marble floor, me skidding
like a fish as we thrashed in my menses,
and the proud mark I bore, see, bruises, then
we showered where water flung to the four walls,
drenching the sink, salt-white towels, toilet,

in that bare Santorini bathroom,
nothing but sea around—sea   sea   sea   sea,
outside the window.

                    Come back to me,
My splendid furred beast, your curled lip snarling.

Five Terraces

John Welpton (1903-1962)

He terraced the back yard in Berkeley, sweat-drenched, hacking out blackberry vines all that summer. To me he was invisible, just a presence down there somewhere, and at dinner our mother would say, "Girls, isn't it wonderful, daddy terraced the hill today with railroad ties he carried himself."

But is this possible? I know he worked with no one, I know there were railroad ties, because there they remained long after his death, dividing what had been an eroding weed-choked hillside into five terraces. First, at the bottom, the badminton court with its white pagoda where in 1961 Billy kissed me. Then the level of bushes, what kind I don't remember. Then the level I loved, where white spider chrysanthemums spilled their feathery petals and draggled in the mud of October, November. Then the level of apple trees, and finally the level of sundial, roses.

Curt, he ordered my sister and me to pick up fallen apples. And how we hated the sweet stench and squlch of bruised or rotten apples in the tall grasses. How we hated him then for making us touch death, making us pile soft wet slush and squoosh of brown apple flesh in buckets—touch what was not lovely with our nearly adolescent fingers, while our parents did the clean work, pruning: she happy to be near him, holding branches, he lopping and shearing.

I knew him that summer, that fall, and not much longer. One day he was in bed. The house was quiet, darkened. "Daddy strained himself in the heat," our mother said. What, exactly, was wrong, we never knew—or whether it was connected with his collapse one Christmastime, his death the next November.

I know him down there somewhere: after the war, after Japan, after his retirement from the Army, those brief Berkeley years when my parents thought at last they'd have a life together. He chops out weeds, cuts back briars, digs terrace levels and smooths the clay. His muscles rope across his back, sweat stings his eyes, as he hauls the heavy railroad ties, terracing. He makes the earth stand still.

October

Irma Welpton Mitchell (1911— 2003)

1   Poem Where You Are Not

In this bleak radiance of October,
I walk the quiet Mississippi streets
and each leaf—burnished, gleaming—

each scarlet berry or green pecan
on the mottled branches
swells

with the sugars of its leaving.
If the dead could stand forth shining
it would be now.

2   From Your Silence, Iridescence

It is not your voice, this trill
through the thicket
we call *insect, bird,* pulse
that rises unbidden
beyond the pine trees.
The claret of this air's not you,
you do not darken
with the sweetgum leaves
or flicker in the shabby galaxies
of asters, you do not
turn with the year
but are gone and gone
and gone so that I wake,
seeing you once more,
and cry out in the dream
as the dream vanishes, *I don't care*
how sick or grouchy
or ugly you are, I just want to talk to you.
Across the memorial urn's
precise cloisonné waters
the dolphins carry you, the dolphins
guard you as they leap and leap,
greeny blue.
The day you died, the nurse said,
the prism at your window
went crazy, shaking and trembling
with rainbows, all the way
out the door the light
broke.

3   Anti-Elegy

For my husband

These words are like sucked thumbs,
like blankets
I wrap around my head.
I mourn my mother, you mourned yours—

That April afternoon your mother's coffin
buzzed and nearly shook with rage
at the rabbi's pieties.
Fuck the "price above rubies," her virtue

did not sustain her. Nor mine; how she wanted
to live. Like our sick black cat,
who craves the food that convulses him, who screams
and paws his throat until he finally learns

it's useless, learns to shun water,
creeps behind the stereo speaker. I'm willing
to say death's a gift. But how lonely, to wait—
then afterward, to shift and mumble grief's bones.

4   Those Hours

I didn't miss you, had got so used
to your dying, wept *goodbye   goodbye*
goodbye   as I left Peace Haven
where you lay three years watching
then barely watching then not watching
the light through that big oak tree
where once you saw a dog
just standing in the grass
outside your window—

where the Christian Science practitioner
prayed for you
and when my sister said,
halting, that we were ready,
we wanted you to be able to die,
he didn't need to keep trying
to heal you, he answered,
"For a year, now,
I've been praying she could go."

—I turned the Honda away
and on to the freeway,
back to Mississippi, eight times
I said goodbye to you, each time
it clenched, ripped.
                        If I could
split wide open, I'd give the world
your small wet self again,
blood-streaked and screaming—

5   What I'm Good At, Sweetest Mama

Flutesong rising like smoke from that 2 a.m. window,
October, the 1960's, San Francisco,
my fingertips tracing circles across my belly
as I listened—up to the heart and down, down,
they called it *effleurage* at the home for unwed mothers
and I thought it meant *flowering*. The sleeping city, the stranger,
his drowsy riff down the street somewhere—
in my bed where Jennifer Lisa ripened toward stillbirth,
I gathered joy with my fingers, stroked joy like petals
into a heap that was the mound of her, as she shifted, floated,
curved me, carved me. You were always afraid for my suffering.
Always afraid *of* my suffering. Now, on your trolley,
you're the queen, the silence; I stroke your hair, dare to kiss
your widow's peak, your lips, one last time I anoint you
with carnation cologne as I used to do when I'd visit,
three drops for you, three drops for me—
                                        What I do best,
I guess, is idolatry. When I caress you on the trolley,
beneath the sheet you are bone, your starved hands
and legs and pelvis already skeletal, your nose and cheekbones
arrogant. Once again I am gathering petals.
Like smoke the flutesong wanders toward oblivion.

6   Homing

The gingko by the sidewalk
has dropped its fruit
and the air is rank
with the squashed globes' stink.
Look at the man
who labors with his bike,
the brown-haired boy
who carries a guitar—
a Jeep, an SUV glide by,
a black dog gallops.
There's always something.

Ladybug ladybug fly away home

Look at the pumpkins,
the bronze chrysanthemums.
A bird sits on the wire.
The pearly evening
spreads around him.

Grief. I bite down hard.

But the Bodhisattva Comes

But the bodhisattva comes
to teach us the path through suffering.
So why would my black cat
not get stuck on the roof
and cry for a week, while all the time
I thought he was under the house
refusing to come out? Why would he not
convulse and retch when I offer him
food or water, not leap away from my
milk-dabbed finger, and when I called
the vet to come over and put him to sleep
why would he not sense it, run to the woods,
stay out in the rain, making it clear to me
he wanted to die in his own way, his own time?
Though I thought it would happen
in a day or two, a week later he is still alive
without water, croaking out to me from what
I know now is the roof—and when at last
I find him, coax him, bring him in
and hold him in my arms, he forgives
me instantly, doesn't he, his spine sticking up
like a tent spine, ribs sunken, fur still sleek
and clean. He lies in my lotus lap and purrs,
kneads, purrs, my thin black cat whose belly
used to drag the ground, whose mouth gives out
the smell of death, cat I've always called
a bodhisattva, because he means nothing but
kindness, big old tomcat nothing but love.
Now he drinks milk again, maybe he'll

pull through. If not now it will be later.
He lies in my lap, and for an instant
I glimpse something very large
through the purring dying creature,
something that blesses us.

Snabbt Jagar Stormen Våra År

"Suddenly a storm hunted down our year"
        —a headstone in a graveyard, Uppsala, Sweden

Suddenly a storm hunted down our year.
And when I raised my head from the table
every leaf lay in the grass. The grass
dazzled. In that piercing blue silence
a door stayed open, holding its breath. Blunt shoes
still with mud on them stood in the closet.

—You hear the quiet voices everywhere.
He was a good husband.   She was a good
sister.   When my first child died I.   Then the
phone rang, they said come, Herr Olsen has fallen.
—They are not a people who show feelings.
You ask them how it goes. *Lagom*, they say;

It means *just enough*. It's how they want their lives
to spin steadily off the skein of new
milky wool. It's how they smile at April's
sticky leaves, how they walk by the Fyris River
each May, photographing the kings'-blood-lilies.
You will not see, when they lose everything.

Kisses

First kiss is Denis Honeychurch, at the party where Jennifer Miles is smooching her no-count boyfriend, C. B. "C. B.?" the girl asks, "Is that his real name?" "Jeez," Jennifer groans, world-weary. "S-E-A-B-E-E. Don't you know it's like a sailor?" They're up, down, up, down, in the clinch on the couch, and each time Jennifer comes up for air she tells the girl, "You've been Denis's girlfriend for months, just *do* it." The girl's ducking this way and that, he's trying to zone in, and finally she lets him and lets him and lets him till her braces are cutting his lips and Jennifer Miles is pulling them apart, bug-eyed, telling her, "Stop now. I won't take *any* responsibility."

Second kiss is Billy McKay at the bottom of the hill that's her back yard. In the little pagoda by the cracked badminton court her father is reclaiming, Billy wraps his arms around her and barely brushes his lips on hers. Nights, she languishes on her balcony, gazes at his roof, imagines him adding her name to the list of the girls he's kissed. She's fourteen. She longs to elope with him to Alaska. The third, fourth, fifth kisses are Billy too. Karl Heimlich calls him no good, tells him to leave her alone, so Billy's friends from St. Mary's storm the school grounds one lunchtime to fight with Karl's friends from Garfield Junior High. "So *this* is the face that launched a thousand fists," Mr. Wigaman, Boys' Dean and history teacher, comments after he breaks the fight up and comes to class.

No, Merrie Lu is earlier than Denis, even. They lie in her bed in the little stucco house upstairs from the shrunken father and bossy Christian Scientist mother who waves her arms around while reciting the Lord's Prayer, and pretend they are grownups. Merrie Lu will take a lover while still in high school—the middle-aged hippie jeweller in the tiny store on Telegraph. She'll vanish from the girl's life, vanish from the circle of girlfriends or even the gossip at Berkeley High. Back then, they put

Kleenex between their lips as they take turns lying on top, lowering their faces toward each other, but they do not touch each other's skin—they're saving their glistening flesh for boys.

Allan Hance is the taste of Chesterfields and boredom. Not boredom with her, just boredom, stretching out blond and lanky on the daybed in his sister's house, kissing hours, hours, as Alicia and her lover and their roommate discuss Nietzsche or béarnaise or their architecture projects in the Berkeley kitchen over *egri bikaver*, bull's-blood wine. In the warm still night, his boredom seems holy. It's not love that's missing between them, but the will to claim, to bind. They don't date, really, just kiss. Like hay ripening, or the stars that make their way across the window, or two corks bobbing on the water, they drift through the months. They'll write for a while, then seldom think of each other again—until he writes her nearly forty years later. There is no end, no end, of things in the heart. He and Alicia are kind to the girl all summer.

It's always easier not to start than to stop, once she parts her lips she's a goner. That consent of the teeth and tongue, the wet, the source of words. When she's small, she knows it makes a wet spot, so she sidles up to some beloved adult—her mother, say, or her mother's best friend Lureen—parts her lips, and touches just the tip of her tongue to the face. In college, she can never understand girls who set out to kiss—to kiss but *just* to kiss—like Kathy Nye in the freshman dorm, who plays the bases like a nun nymphomaniac. If the girl kisses someone she wants his body in hers, to hurl herself over all the steeplejack jumps. The *yes* is nearly infinite.

And when she is grown, kissing her children, she wants to bless them with her lips, to seal them forever in her love. Eskimo kisses where they rub noses, trading breath, "Nuggie nose, nuggie nose." Butterfly kisses—eyelashes tickling the cheek, up and down, fluttering. Eating the toes and fingers kisses, smunching down on the belly kisses. Kisses on the eyes to magic away headaches, on the salty sweat-damp hair, the hollow under the ear, the plump pulse at the clavicle. Kisses like water sheeting down a mountainside. Kisses like birth fluid, floating them, surrounding them, until the day they die. No, confess. She wants her kiss-shaped burning seal still to be glowing at the end of eternity.

Rain

Rain is the music she listens to as, sleepless, she wanders around the house, trying to find a place to settle—bathtub, living room, guest room, kitchen. This is the practice of the night; it began last winter, almost a year ago. She wakes keeping watch with a duple heart, which splits to flower, like a dicotyledon. She wakes in love and trouble of mind. *Ann Ann* she calls herself, practicing in silence the Buddhist doubling exercise she read about, to shake the attention loose from the bound identity. *Ann   Ann* —She becomes both the caller and answerer. *Yes I'm coming* she replies.

Night gathers in the kitchen, along the counters, and the rain pours down. The clock on the stove shines fluorescent, 2:39, 2:40, as the ceiling fan pushes the cool wet air. Rain drenches every inch of the garden, turns the dust to September mud again, gives the passion flower new energy for vining. Her husband sleeps in their bed; his skin is on fire and his soft snores ratchet. Again and again she has tried to sleep, has curved against his back, her leg across his hip. Again and again she has dozed, and waked.

There is a man—her boyfriend from forty years ago. He vanished more completely than rain, it wasn't his fault, just one of those things. He's back in her life, he's a doctor in Paris. And when she wakes she thinks, *my waking is his sleeping, my midnight is his morning.* Now he's at work. He's had his *pain de mie* and chicory coffee, he's walked down the Avenue St. Ouen past the outdoors market with its vivid jumble of meats and fruits, past the *Ivoiriens* shouting their greetings to Africa in the phone booths, where he calls her sometimes.

70

She has words for the others. *Husband, friend, child...* But what do you call a man you love, a man who loves you, who is not your husband and not—because of your husband, his wife—your lover? Not *my love*, and not *my other love* either. Not *sweetheart*, she doesn't quite dare. Not, God forbid, *my temptation.* Though she's been tempted.

My lost one. My found.

Hearing the Mass in French Again

I came in off the street to check my map,
thinking that in a church
thieves would not find me.
Fifteen women, mostly old,
murmured the responses
where a priest and boy presided
over a nest of shadows. Dark stone,
noon in Paris but the city silent.
And hearing the words in French
comforted me;
I heard them first
in Liège, thirty-five years ago,
where the orphans' thin blue jackets
rustled like birds' wings as they knelt
all together in the freezing chapel,
then filed to take Communion.

Comforted me because
I was present before this misery.

Dawn spills like milk across the dirty Paris sky
outside my window.

Again today
I will ask God in whom I must believe
what he wants of me: "must," because I keep
talking to him: God, what am I doing,
visiting this man?
Why do I feel this way?
How long must I walk before my body

tires and I can slink back to a room
which is not mine, which will never be mine—
the room where his son grew up, where his wife
keeps red geraniums—
and lie on the bed and watch the swallows
as they fly up, up, across the pale sky—
anywhere in the world, just out of here.

Having No Choice, I Welcome You

To Kali, to the Dirty Lady

Come barefoot.

      Come with your hair down
            in your skirt of knives.

            Come through the rain.

Come to me where the wind blows—

      Here on the Allée Marcel Proust
            where voices rise on the currents of air,
                where sunlight is a bird
            and the sawing, down the Rue Royale, of sirens.
     You only do not die, though the woman
            in russet stockings strolling with her man
                and her leather shoulderbag, and the woman
            who limps already, and the salsa dancer
  who carries his shoulders unmoving
            and leads with his black-clad hips must die,
                all of us in this wind, and the great,
            wind-whipped chestnut trees.

      Each angle and tumble of hair, each stride,
            like that man with the swagger and sway,
                or the black man in linen, the woman
            with her head down who carries
  a Gucci shopping bag—each pigeon
            cutting the air—
                and the fragility of their wishes,

their cheekbones—

I accept you into my heart
      but you have no comfort for me.

Come to me, come to me,
        you with the crimson.

When the World Opens Its Petals

He is muttering to the Seine.

Rail-thin, like a heron,
on a bollard,
he wears an indigo shirt,
white pants with indigo stains.
His lips never stop moving,
though the sky grows stormy,
the water choppy.

A nearly empty tour boat passes.
He pays no attention
to its tinkly waltzes.

       * * *

This is the one day ever
you and I will walk through the Marais,
buy crickets for your chameleon,
then head down to the river—

the one day we'll walk slowly,
my hand in the crook of your arm,
nearly as if we're permitted.

The world opens its bittersweet petals.

I stop to watch him. You go
a little further,
then stop to watch me.

However far he's come,
whatever he's telling the Seine,
he is part of our aloneness.

76

L'Empire de l'Amour

If you enter a house where there has been
good loving, they have changed their clothes
since you last saw them, and maybe their eyes
are sleepy, or they have washed their hair. She
curls like a cat on the leather couch,
reading the paper as he stirs onions
in the kitchen. Red wine warms in their glasses
as Chopin rises, and she says, "who, I wonder,
is our Chopin now, and who our George Sand?"

If the man who now stirs onions in the kitchen
held you for five minutes earlier that morning
in the Cimetière de Montmartre—held you quietly
because you love each other though you are not
having an affair—and then to clear out
of their way because he is after all
her husband, you walked all day around the Louvre

(poor you, walking all day around the Louvre
while your own warm husband who caresses you
in the middle of the night and tells you stories
about the dog who got lost in the forest
and vanquished the robbers, and loves how you smell—
while your own warm, twenty years' husband
holds down the fort back home as you live this out)—

If you enter this house, you need
to pull yourself up by the nape's short hairs,
pray not to cause, but to accept, this pain,
remembering how suffering blazed out
in the Metro, where getting off the train

you suddenly heard the violinist
lost in the middle of Bach's "Ave Maria,"
and you stood there with your eyes closed, weeping—
and remembering how suffering blazed out
among all those medieval paintings
of tormented bodies, and Caravaggio,

the Death of the Virgin, such a beautiful woman
not to have known the mortal flesh of a man.
She lay on a bed, head toward you, body
stretching away from you, one hand flung out,
hair a nest of shadows, as men
gathered in the darkness watching her.
Her other hand rested near her womb—

Split fruit, a lake of fire. God's lily.

Mississippi

1

Since Friday a small white cat has lain on the sidewalk next to Inside Oxford. Ants crawl in its fur, ichor pools around its nostrils. Soon, that sweet smell will rise as it bloats in the heat and stiffens further. Drive by it, drive back at the end of the day. No one has removed it. Drive by again next morning, then, in the evening, walk up close to look at it. Its eyes have spread from temple to temple, as if someone had laid the blue wings of a Morphos butterfly tenderly across it.

2

Kudzu's ragged emerald
          splays across the gully

stormclouds hover
          a bumblebee stumbles through grasses
                    sucks the thick yolk of magnolias

tiretracks ripple
          in mud beneath your feet
                    shadowy cedars loom at dream's torn selvage

a spiderweb pearls with rain
          gnats drink from your eyes
                    the daddy long legs totes his sac of poison

wet, now, the trail you take
                  birdsong dissolving

wet like your gristle and tendons
                wet like the secrets and needs of you

3

Downtown, every lily has its place,
every hydrangea fertilized for pink
or blue, tamped down beneath pine straw,

geometrically arranged. The manicured clumps
of monkey grass, barberry mounds, crape myrtles
on the curb like sixth-grade ballroom dancing

when I waited for a boy to cross the floor—
puffy, in magenta polished cotton.
Oh I wish something would lash out, some tendril

slip its moorings and strangle care in us.
By the brick Arts Center that leveled half a hill
of kudzu, snakes, and shadows,

the bronze fiddler advertises
(with her dirty feet stamping and her
hair flying) "wildness." Nights, my husband

turns to me but it's too hot to touch.
Once we braved just about anything—
I danced for him, I danced for him.

The ceiling fan sluggishly churning.

4

Last winter in Uppsala, Sweden,
seven months into our year, I saw a crumpled
scrap of paper on the stairs to the apartment.
In that city with its birch trees
and the rushing Fyris River,
I thought it was a cockroach, and was
happy. I said "*Damn*, that's home, I live there."
For the first time I missed Oxford—
where in summer, by the Jitney,
streams of roaches from the gutter
ferry all night long, scrabbling into Lethe.

5

Once, we were in the same city—
this man who drifted away
when I was eighteen,
who found me again nearly forty years later.

His wife, my husband,
waited, chatting of schools or Strindberg,
back home in the apartment.
I held his elbow up Draggarbrunnsgatan
to the ICA, where we debated
about chicken, yoghurt, cherries, moving slowly
and more slowly, wanting it to take exactly forever.

The flatbread and pickled herring
shone with a holy light
as we stumbled along the aisles, clutching our little red baskets.

6

This wet and heavy summer
makes the soil rich.
Love brings the women dreams of peaches.

I get the car home, drunk. In the driveway
an orange zinnia is blossoming.
My husband stands in the kitchen, twirling
a tinsel pinwheel he has brought home
from his rambles in the woods.
The crystal decanter we bought in Calico Rock
on our fifteenth anniversary
glows on the table like a thousand rubies.

A kid trails down the street, holding a Coke can.
My son sways on the porch swing,
his old Great Dane with the swollen paws
sprawled beneath him.

7

I can't outwalk myself. Streetlights, moonlight—
          down Price, up Sivley—
When I get to Annandale, there it is.
          Creature of tongues, it watches from shadows.

It tells me, Take off your skin,
          your sound and sight,
unwind these sheets, and dance for me.
          Dance for me.

It tells me, Night across the pond thickens
         where the owl is riding.
You'll be the hare caught in its claws,
         fear and fur, a skittering meat thing.

8

It's whipping up storm tonight.
The rusted Hindu temple bells on the porch sing.

I tell myself,
         I have come back to Mississippi—
to the mud daubers' swollen, intricate chambers,

the spiders' parchment egg sacs,
the soft throng of their new-hatched babies.

I tell myself,
         I have come back to the place where I will die—

My kind husband, on his side, stretches out his arms to me.
But where I am, not even the cicadas chanting in the thicket know.

A Confession

"And you too, God—you are ill with me."

That was a bad BLT day. Full summer, when the magnolia leaves hang leathery, cicadas scrape at my brain with their incessant crescendos of chanting and whirring, and sweat stinks up my clothes so bad I need to shower three times a day. And exhaustion sets in: I'm like Scobie's wife in *The Heart of the Matter*, I just want to lie beneath a mosquito net and whine.

So when I made BLT's for supper I didn't toast the bread, ciabatta, which was soggy. I used overripe tomatoes, and undercooked the bacon and overmayoed the bread. My husband got pissed, really pissed, because he too is living in a climate where the underwear is rank and the blood sugar is zero. And he said, *I'm not going to tell you this is a good dinner, and I'm not going to eat it.*

I slammed off in the car, and drove out of Oxford toward the Waterfowl Refuge, seeking dark, seeking silence, when a deer came bounding into the front wheel of my Honda. I felt the thud, I sickened, there was the *gimp leap gimp leap* as the tormented animal lurched bounding away across the fields, and back across the lightless road that ran alongside kudzu and beaten-down trailers.

Now the front of my Honda is dented where the hot flank hit it. Swear to God, I couldn't do but evil in the Mississippi summer.

The River

1

They looked back across the river at the simplest things that had once been theirs. The mysterious huts stood open and lighted on the other side of the water. And in the huts were bowls of milk they had set aside. A dog lay sleeping, curled around a boy, whose face was wet with tears. On the far riverbank, candles lit the path beside the water.

They looked back across the river at the cups they had held once in their hands, the clothes piled on chairs, soft white and red or dusky blue that had once warmed them, that they had touched once with rough fingers. Looked at the low wood beds, the bread on plates, a flute and shoe abandoned in a corner.

They would do anything, give anything, not to have to turn their heads away. Where they looked back across the river, birds nested in the blue branches that the sun had painted but that rustled now in darkness, each leaf whole, each leaf connected.

And those shining little huts, with the milk still warm in bowls, breathed in the darkness.

2

And the quaking aspens?

Wherever they touched, they shivered.

3

No, I cannot tell you where they are going when they have crossed the river. You must answer that yourself.

Make a roommate out of dust.
Closing your eyes, recall where you have been loneliest.

Then take the first step on to the paths that branch forever.

VI

In That Kitchen

She fed so many children for so many years. *Can I pour you some milk?*
Would you like some peach pie? Tch, no one ate them and now the
bananas have blackened. Now it's come down to two sons, home for the
moment. And the one, 19, sleeps all day and parties all night; he mostly
just wants fast food, even when he's said what she could cook for him.
And the other, 25, works construction, comes home covered with dust
and sweat and sometimes too tired to eat, sits smoking on the porch for
hours, staring off into the leaves, his Great Dane on the dog-smelling
cushion beside him. The boys are healthy, yes, but they smoke too much
and eat too little, their chests and ribs are bony. She's laying down food
that doesn't get eaten, though her husband tries. Some nights it's so hot
the thought of food sickens, and all they want is fritos or beer or those ice
cream sandwiches from Kroger, mint ice cream between chocolate
cookies.

So the ceiling fan churns slowly. The windows her older son painted, like
bits of Aegean Sea set in ripply heartpine, are full of summer—redbud,
willow oak, star-shaped leaves of the maple they planted five years ago,
spreading leaves of the gingko they planted twelve years ago. The trees
flash scarlet with the liquid calls of cardinals. It's August in that kitchen.
Surrounded by silent men, her life is full of beauty and her life is full of
love, yet she doesn't know where she's going.

Being the mother was a long rapture, a long abandonment. Abandonment
of what? Of herself? Of silence? But how much love can flow through
your hands, *did* flow through her hands, into the cakes, the pies, the
sandwiches and stews. And thence into their bones, their bodies. It's
quiet now. Her husband reads, her sons are heading out for the night.
She's dying to ask her menfolk if they'd like some quesadillas.

Point Reyes

1

The grey ghost rises on the wind,
splitting the air with his harrying cry.
Great blue herons stalk the tule marshes.
Already, fog gathers on the waters.
It will swell to a spill along Inverness Ridge,
the houses across the water will disappear,
even our own feet will grow cold
and shadowy beneath us. We are spume
on a single wave, a wave that comes to shore
between one foghorn and the next,
and Trinket knows this, that's why she wants
the Sailor, she dreams he will have the roll of the sea
in his thighs, the forgetfulness
of the sea behind his eyes, in his fingers.

2

You whose fingers on this white page
trace their blue scratches and loops in a language
called English, writing where the fog
thickens and rolls in, blotting out the sun
across the mesa . . . You in whom darkness
flows through all your organs and bones
and just beyond your eyes, beneath the infinite
skin of the world . . . You whose hand, here
with its two moonstone thumb rings,
its crackly warm terrain of skin and knuckles
and tendons, its pink polished fingernails,

90

is a moment's stiff or agile knot
of bones and flesh and *prana* . . . Even now,
as three geese in formation fly overhead
and mist or small rain begins to fall
on the last single-petalled crimson roses,
you move from beauty into beauty.

3

The cricket laps at the night like a cat laps cream.
Grains and knots of this burnished desk wood
flow like the rivers of sand at Limantour Beach,
where I saw a man with feathers, once.
I'd broken away from the boy who tried to kiss me
in the dunes, and walked on down the beach
far from the hot dogs and lemonade.
The man with feathers was dancing, this was 1963.
He croaked and warbled, slowly spiralling up,
up, up, his scrawny arms and fingers
stretching out so wide he held the sky. He scared me.
But I wish I'd gone to sit near him, to watch him
as I idly stroked the warm driftwood, the long
bulbous sea kelp that lay in the luminous sand—
or rise to my feet and begin to dance with him.

At McClure's Beach, Point Reyes National Seashore, California

I would ask my family

Wait for a foggy afternoon, late May,
after a rainy winter so that all
the wildflowers are blooming on the headland.
Wait for honey of lupine. It will rise
around you, encircle you, from vast golden bushes
as you take the crooked trail
down from the parking lot. Descend
earth's cleft, sweet winding declivity
where California poppies lift up their
chalices, citrine and butterscotch,
and phlox blows in the wisps of fog, every
color of white and like the memory
of pain, and like first dawn, and lavender.
Where goldfinches, nubbins of sunlight,
flit through the canyon. Walk one by one
or in small clusters, carrying babies,
children holding your hands—with your eyes,
your oval skulls, your prodigious memories
or skills with the fingers. Your skirts or shirts
will flirt with the wind, and small brown rabbits
will run in and out, you'll see their ears first,
nested in the grasses, then the bob
of fleeting hindquarters.
     Now come to the sand,
the mussel shells, broken or open, iridescent,
color of crows' wings in flight
or purple martins, and the bullwhips

of sea kelp, some like frizzy-headed voodoo
poppets, some like long hollow brown or bleached
phalluses. The X X birdprints running
across the scalloped sand will leave a trail of stars,
look at the black oystercatcher, the scamp
with the long red beak, it's whizzing along
in its courtship dance. Look at the fog,
above you now on the headland, and know how much
I love the fog. Don't cry, my best beloveds,
it's time to scatter me back now. I've wanted this
all my life. Look at the cormorants,
the gulls, the elegant scythed whimbrel,
do you hear its *quiquiquiquiqui*
rising above the eternal Ujjayi breath,
the roar and silence and seethe and whisper,
the immeasurable insweep and release of ocean.

When You Come to Love

When you come to love,
bring all you have.

Bring the milk in the jug,
the checked cloth on the table—
the conch that sang the sea
when you were small,
and your moonstone rings,
your dream of wolves,
your woven bracelets.

For the key to love is in the fire's nest,
and the riddle of love
is the hawk's dropped feather.

Bring every bowl and ewer,
every cup and chalice, jar,
for love will fill them all—

And, dazzled with the day,
fold the sunlight in your sheets,
fold the smell of salt and leaves,
of summer, sweat, and roses,
to shake them out when you need them most,

For love is strong as death.

Marriage

I dream my husband naked in the mountains
in summer his unabashed groin
lovely to my gaze a split pomegranate.

Crimson with seeds he sprawls on a boulder
his groin a darkness a kiss
I know in my sleep pomegranate is a female metaphor

but I mean he teaches me mystery.

I don't know anything about marriage, our son says.
Twenty years in the same bed sleeping waking
your thoughts all tangled up in each other . . .

Night opens her dress
the great winds of the world
arrange themselves for storm outside our window.

I pull the quilts around us closer.

That such a one as he should ever die—

He dreams I write of the bareness of winter.

Dream Cabinet

A quail's nest, two blown eggs.
Eyeglasses blue as the sea off Thasos
where on their honeymoon they'll dive
and find the donkey's skull, carry
it back to France and then America—
it will decay and stink, never finally
clean, on a stone patio as crickets chirr
in the bamboo, in California. Finally
dogs will carry it to the mountains.
Sleek claws of vulture and raven,
globed coral lobed and branching,
pink scrap of silk slip
stained with the sweat and grease paint
of her Sailor. Book streaked with erasures,
diary without days . . .

        And bicycle wheels.
The god's blue handprints. Three black plums
on a stone white plate. A vortex of stars,
a supernova. A child's high-buttoned shoe
and the photograph of a child,
her shadowy unborn face as she swims,
hair lifting forever like slow feathers,
toward you.

In the Manner of the Long Married

Terror of what I long for most, that passion,
breaking open, like the exposed flesh of a shell-crushed snail
glistening, in mortal anguish: this I want,
to lie all open.
On the phone I can feel your body; it wants me, not just for sex,
but for salt and sleep and bread.
Your hair's gray now, all but the eyelashes—

                    We sat on the porch, once,
in Charlottesville,
all through the storm. The rain beat sideways
and we drank red wine, put our feet up on the rail. We were drenched
but it didn't matter, then, or on the night we slept
in the tent you called "clammy." By flashlight I bailed water with your shoe
and we fought about Blake, whether it's better to murder an infant
than nurse unacted desire. I still don't know.

                    When I'm with you I'm shy
in the manner of the long married,
but talking to you on the phone these seventeen days
I feel the whole length of your body.
We are just the right height for each other, I tip and curve my spine
to touch you everywhere.

                    Why terror?
You've washed our white sheets, you've swept and put out flowers
to welcome me home. No matter how far I fall
through the water you'll be there;
the hawk screams its strange harsh scream and plunges and you'll be
smiling at me at the end of it.
Then you'll know what you already know.

Sphinx, Star-Gazer, Mountain

Leading yoga. For Beth Ann Fennelly

1

Beth Ann, don't grieve,
the year that I'll be gone goes quickly.
Cicadas will clamor in the cedars
and the chiggers run amok,
little Claire will be perfecting
Throwing-Fits-in-the-Grocery-Store,
if she's anything like mine she'll hit *No* early.
Flushed with Chianti and your five-years'-anniversary-trip
to Florence, you'll be starting another baby. We'll practice yoga,
you in your skin-tight body suit, me in my ratty p.j. pants
and one or another tank top with the scarlet bra straps showing.
Maybe my hip will be better, maybe I'll have that
legs-in-tailor-fashion-torso-flat-on-the-ground
flexibility back again. Maybe your Downward Dog
will be all the way down, head and heels both tenting you.
Who knows?

Breathe deep, Beth Ann,
you're like pennies from heaven.

2

Push back
into Downward Facing Dog, press away with your hands,
lift the pelvis, let the heels melt toward the ground,
spread your fingers, breathe, breathe,
let Ujjayi breath roar up through your throat

and flower in your stout heart, you are learning
to carry the ocean. Lead with the heart
as you arc up and back in Star-gazer, lead with the heart,
let your homage to night and all the starry rivers
bring you over, head bowing down toward your front knee,
hands twisted all the way back to lift, palms together,
behind you . . .
        Sorrow covers the globe.
As you face earth you see how sorrow
sifts in the dust, *we wait for rain,*
for football, for justice, sorrow chokes the dried creekbeds.
My husband at the table in our 100-year-old house
reads me the words of Arundhati Roy—
Are you writing another book? Another book?
Right now? ...What kind of book should I write?
My favorite student Isaac comes to class,
I don't recognize him, he's been called up
from inactive reserve, has a military buzz cut.
We're going to Iraq, he says, any day now.
He's 22, skinny and smart like my sons. The Marines
has made him a pacifist. I'm trying to teach Elizabeth Bishop,
your favorite poet, and I'm stunned, stalled. It's going to take
guys like me dying, he says, not being in class, before this country
stops to think. Class, what does it mean,
More delicate than the historians' are the map-makers' colors?
What colors are the historians'? They think. Silence.
Then: Black and white?
Red?

3

Lying on the belly, place the hands before you, arms bent,
elbows close to the body.
Lift into Sphinx and gaze out level across the desert.

Now stand with the feet together or close, parallel,
toes spread wide, all four points of the foot grounding, strong,
earth holds you. Draw up through the calves,
wrap the thighs to the bone, drop the pelvis,
open the chest, the belly is soft, the shoulders are back and down.
This is Mountain. Here you can stay, touching earth and sky.
                                        Breathe.
                            Follow the breath.
                Just follow the breath.
Let the thoughts grow calm.

Your face after yoga when you see Claire
is all the birds at dawn
in the trees outside my window. *Trouble is coming,
trouble is all around,* and I wish for you
the heart a flower,
                at its center a golden fountain.

VII

Walking Wu Wei's Scroll
"Le Grand Fleuve à perte de vue"

But the faintest pink in the houses to the left—
                                                    is that dawn,
or has someone lit some tiny lanterns?

                    *   *   *

Here and there, all facing the same direction,
fishing boats near and far: alone, together.

And half the people walking this scroll
here at the Grand Palais on the 21st of June
move left to right, and half move right to left.
It doesn't matter.

No climax, no conclusion.

We begin with such solidity: large trees, boulders,
thickest and densest at the beginning.
Midway through the scroll, the emptiness is greatest,
the *brume* thickest. Then, moving left, the solidity returns.

But no: moving left, the emptiness returns.
The village fades away once more, at the left side of the scroll,

and we're in fog, in swirl and fade,
with only the faintest shadows to say "mountain"
and slashes to say "foreground: trees,"
or maybe "boats," or maybe just "slashes."

*   *   *

Where would I be in this? I would be anywhere.

Each thing singular, each thing perfect,
fog and water
and tree and rocks, the fish that swims in its bowl,
the blood that swims in the bowl of the body.
Entrails, cilia—and here, toward the left side of the scroll,
the faintest touches of pink:

Why? As if dawn is coming?

And here again, a village, two men on a bridge,
the torque and slow fluidity of trees.

Brushstrokes black on gray
define the ridges of the mountains.

                    *   *   *

Ah, the courage to leave something empty.
To wait, and wait,
                        and wait,
as the hair-thin fishing boats float and wait

                    till at last, the world (as we call it)
reconstitutes itself in the solemnity of boulders.
As on both sides of the scroll—
to east, to west; to right, to left—
solidity cups fog, or as two hands cup the silence where a face was.

Now we have come to the place,
my love,
where I must lay you down.
Only a few hair-thin scribbles of boats endure,
and the mountains
whose edges cannot be distinguished from shadow.

*   *   *

Time mars the silk:
a few spots and stains, as if smoke or tears.
Then rushes, fishing junks, elegant curved sails,
facing into the open waters.

And what do *you* want? Where is your house?
Or do you walk among the rocks, beneath the trees?

Oh, me, if I can't be the fish,
swimming giddily round and round as my orange fins
flashed and his hands warmed my waters,
then I'd like to be the fog,
and lay my touch down
on every crack and crevice, every pine,
every boulder—and give the villagers sleep.

* * *

Now they go down to boats we do not see.
The merest wisps of pine trees dot the waters.

Somewhere in those houses, a lover turns to his beloved.
Somewhere else, a child cries.

But the cries
of their pain or pleasure are lost in the fog…
though not how a man's hands caress
and caress a blue bowl, turning and warming it
between his fingers—
a bowl in which a fish, now dizzy with circling, swims.

*   *   *

Out of silence, the brimming lake, spills the waterfall.
Behind mountains, other mountains fade
until we cannot tell
what's stone, what's cloud,
and what the mark of time upon the silk.

And look, here someone rides home—
or is it a squiggle—
up the path to a terraced house.
Then a village fading in fog,
on the watery side of the mountain.

You could be that aspen, that cedar—
or the woman we do not see, who spins thread or boils silkworms
in the house below the boulder, the house
of which we see
an upper roof corner, and another, then the rocks surround it.

*　*　*

You could be the man in the small house making tea,
or one of the friends fishing off the footbridge over the river.

Notes

Walking Wu Wei's Scroll *"Le Grand Fleuve à perte de vue"*

Wu Wei, 1459-1509, lived during the Ming Dynasty. This room-length horizontal scroll was on display at the Grand Palais in Paris, in the exhibit of "Montagnes célestes" during the spring and early summer of 2004. Translated from the French translation from the Chinese, the title means, approximately, "the great river as far as the eye can see," or, more evocatively, "the great river to the loss of sight or view."

The Trinket Poems

From the preface to the poems, by Michele Cuomo

"The Mutilated" was first presented as part of a double bill entitled *The Slapstick Tragedy*, which its author Tennessee Williams described as "a wildly idiomatic sort of tragedy," at the Longacre Theatre, New York, on February 22, 1966. It closed after only seven performances. The original *New York Times* review by Stanley Kauffmann, on February 23, 1966, saw no evidence of transcendence in the work, just a drunken vision, a "glandular and alcoholic religiosity."

In April 2002 I directed a production of *The Slapstick Tragedy* at the University of Mississippi, featuring Ann Fisher-Wirth as Trinket Dugan in "The Mutilated." Trinket's left breast has been removed. Her mutilation leaves her heart close to the surface. Celeste, her shoplifting prostitute companion, "exposes" Trinket's mutilation, not only by scratching it on the bathroom wall, but also by slowly opening her heart. Trinket at first seeks to salve her wound with "the Christmas gift of a lover." In our production, Trinket adorned herself with Mardi Gras beads and stretched them out to her drunken sailor, offering herself as a

111

sacrifice in a Dionysian ritual; she returned to the spirit of the original Mardi Gras carnival, a valediction to *carne*, offering herself to indulge the sailor's desire to rend her further. This ritual, however, is a failure, as the sailor and Trinket tear away from each other when Celeste's screams interrupt them, and the sailor falls asleep. Trinket is then stirred by maternal longings, and mourns her missing breast for its ability to nourish. She transfers her desire back to the maternal, and feeds and comforts the starving, childlike Celeste. She passes wine and wafer to Celeste, and in that ritual of the mass, her room at the Silver Dollar Hotel becomes a sacred space where Trinket and Celeste can commune with the divine.

Butoh, the subject of the final poem in the series, was born out of a reaction against the devastation of Hiroshima and Nagasaki. The butoh dancer seeks to commune with the dead and suffering, to take the body to a crisis point, which then becomes a meditation on the body and the spirit. It is a dance form with roots in theatre traditions; theorist Antonin Artaud and actor/director Jean Louis Barrault influenced its founders. It also borrows from traditional Japanese performance styles to contextualize body, time, and space. Butoh movement mixes the material and the spirit. For instance, a dancer finding "The Bird," a movement sequence by Min Tanaka, seeks to embody the spirit of Bird, to discover its nature through the dance, "to live the question of life and death." (Tomoe)

Have we become so mutilated, have we amputated spirit from our daily existence, or are we ready to become butoh artists, moving our bodies and spirits as one? Can we see the most sacred moments in the most profane spaces? Can we see the beauty in "glandular and alcoholic religiosity"? Tennessee Williams in "The Mutilated" celebrates what Ann Fisher-Wirth has named "the holy whore." "The Trinket Poems" invite us to join him in this celebration.

A Confession

"And you too, God—you are ill with me" is a line from Graham Greene's novel *The Heart of the Matter*; Scobie, who writes it, is the novel's protagonist.

Having No Choice, I Welcome You

Kali is the goddess of death in the Hindu pantheon. She is widely worshiped in a variety of guises. The "dirty lady" is Tlazolteotl, the Aztec goddess of filth whose function is similar to Kali's, and who wears a skirt of knives.

Sphinx, Star-Gazer, Mountain

"Sphinx," "Star-Gazer," and "Mountain" are names of yoga poses, as is "Downward Facing Dog." Ujjayi breath, also mentioned in "At McClure's Beach, Point Reyes National Seashore, California," is a powerful, deep inhalation and exhalation taken at the back of the throat; it sounds like the roar of the ocean.

Printed in the United States
43428LVS00009B/184

9 781893 239449